ORGANIZATIONAL CULTURE

A FORCE FIERCE AS FIRE

Harness the **Hidden Hand** of Culture
by Creating an Ethically Intelligent Organization

JOHN T. OPINCAR

Houston, Texas
Copyright © 2017 by John T. Opincar

Houston, Texas
Copyright © 2017 by John T. Opincar

All rights reserved. In accordance with the U. S. Copyright Act of 1976, the scanning, uploading and electronic sharing of any part of this book without permission of the publisher constitute unlawful piracy and theft of the author's intellectual property. If you would like to use material from the book (other than for review purposes), prior written permission must be obtained by contacting the publisher at permissions@culturalfirepress.com.

Thank you for your support of the author's rights.

Cultural Fire Press, LLC
Suite 450
8300 Cypress Creek Parkway
Houston, Texas 77070
www.culturalfirepress.com

Printed in the United States of America

First Edition: April 2017

You may contact the author at john.opincar@boardroompartners.com.

Cover and interior design by Brett Miller, www.bjm-bookdesign.com.

The publisher is not responsible for websites (or their content) that are not owned by the publisher.

Library of Congress Cataloging-in-Publication Data has been applied for.
ISBN: 978-0-9980890-8-9

10 9 8 7 6 5 4 3 2 1

This book is dedicated to the late management guru, Peter Drucker, who said, "Culture eats strategy for breakfast!"

ETHICAL INTELLIGENCE HEADLINES

Here are some significant messages emerging from the world of ethical intelligence research and practice:

- Everything we "know" about ethical decision making is wrong.
- Lying is at the root of all unethical behavior.
- Ethics from the heart beats ethics from the head.
- Organizational wet work kills people and organizations.
- Don't leave your comfort zone.
- Organizational omerta is a path to prison.
- Greed isn't the root of unethical behavior—fear is.
- Success means avoiding the Family of Five Fears.
- Don't become a hostage in the Innocuous Imperial Box.
- The future of leadership is gardening.
- Ingratitude, right behind lying, is at the root of unethical behavior.
- The Sick Six Termites of organizational culture will collapse your organization.
- Clean your worldview window. Dirty windows lead to dirty behavior.
- We can predict and prevent unethical behavior.
- Shoot the messenger! So, you want to be a whistle-blower?
- Do you know who cleans your toilets? You should.
- Slippery slopes have led many to prison.
- Relationships are at the heart of leadership and ethical intelligence.
- Ethical intelligence is measurable and modifiable.
- The Holocaust reaches from the past and touches today's ethical judging.
- You're not doing life alone.
- Leaders should be tested and licensed.
- You cannot lead without ethical intelligence.

Source: Ethical Intelligence Research Center | www.ethicalintelligence.org

CONTENTS

Ethical Intelligence Headlines	iv
About this Book	1
Foundations	3
Ethical Intelligence	3
Human Collective Unconscious	4
The Primal Relationship	5
Our Struggle for Selfhood	5
Introduction	7
Chapter 1: Culture—A Force Fierce As Fire	9
Hidden Hand of Culture	11
Cultural Gestalt	15
Values	17
Myths	20
Artifacts	24
Tradition	26
Culture Dysfunctions	27
Hypocrisy	28
Wet Work	30
Organizational Omerta	33
Toxic Triangle: Arrogance, Hubris and Entitlement	36
Pressure to Perform	38
Shoot the Messenger	42
A Success Story	45
From Strip Clubs and Ladies of the Evening to Family Outings	47
Chapter 2: Ethically Intelligent Organizations	52
Lock the Barn Door	54
Roadmap To An Ethically Intelligent Organization	59
Truth	60

People	62
R² Behaviour	63
Acting	65
Culture	67
Cloister	68
Otherness	70
Reform	71
Foreign Corrupt Practices Act (FCPA)	71
Regulation Full Disclosure (FD)	74
Essential Credential	75

About the Author   77

ABOUT THIS BOOK

This book contains two chapters excerpted from the groundbreaking book—*Ethical Intelligence: The Foundation of Leadership*. The genesis of this brief work is the continuing request from busy managers and leaders who wanted just the information that is reflected in this book's title.

This book answers the following questions:

Question: How do I control behavior in my organization?
Answer: Through your culture.

Question: So then, what is culture?
Answer: Read Chapter 1

Question: Is it powerful enough to control behavior?
Answer: Read Chapter 1

Question: How do I know if my culture is working?
Answer: Read Chapter 1

Question: How do I change it, if it's not?
Answer: By creating an ethically intelligent organization.

Question: What is an ethically intelligent organization?
Answer: Read Chapter 2

Question: How do I create one?
Answer: You begin by creating an R^2 culture.

Question: What's that?
Answer: Right-thinking-right-acting.

Question: How do I do that?
Answer: Begin by reading this brief book. Commit to making the changes.

Then call us, and we'll be glad to help!

BOARDROOM PARTNERS, INC.
World Headquarters: Houston, Texas, USA
www.boardroompartners.com
john.opincar@boardroompartners.com
david.breslauer@boardroompartners.com
346-444-2626

FOUNDATIONS

As you read this brief book, there two sets of terms and four foundational ideas I want to mention for your consideration before we get started. First, the terms decision-making and judging don't refer to the same phenomenon. I am making a decision when I consider the merits of one investment option over another or I choose a place to eat lunch. Judging implies and involves weighing the equity of outcomes in relationships. Judging is about people and relationships. It is reserved for relationships between and among human beings.

Second, Self and Other are philosophical and psychological terms, which can seem off-putting and academic. I use these words throughout the book because they're efficient in conveying precise meanings. The Self is the self-aware, thinking you. The Other is all else. The Other may be an individual, a group or an organization, such as a competitor or governmental agency. Otherness is all that is not you.

Finally, there are four foundational ideas for your consideration: human ethical intelligence, human collective unconscious, our primal relationship, and our struggle for Selfhood. We'll discuss these ideas in Part One, but I want to introduce them here because of their importance. First, we lay out the basic meaning of ethical intelligence.

> **Ethical Intelligence.** Ethical intelligence is the intellectual capacity and framework for judging matters of equity in relationships. It has four separate but integrated elements consisting of (1) relationships, (2) equity, (3) ethical judging

and (4) intellectual capacity and framework. This last element contains seven psychological, neurological, mystical or spiritual structures, as follows: Worldview Window, Heart Refuge, Limbic System, Internal Compass, Ethical Fence, Slippery Slope and Adjudicator. We'll discuss all of this in Part One.

Next, we offer Jung's idea of the human collective unconscious.

Human Collective Unconscious. The idea of human interconnectedness has many names. It was popularized as "the Force" in the Star Wars series of movies. Carl Jung named it the human collective unconscious. I like Jung's description because it's both elegant and consistent with the principles of quantum physics. Jung considered the collective unconscious the common inheritance of humanity, a kind of reservoir of human thoughts and experiences that has existed since the beginning.

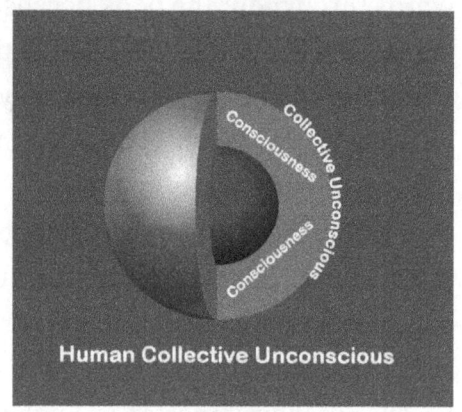

Human Collective Unconscious

This reservoir is available to all of us, and when something happens anywhere it's happened everywhere. I've captured my personal visualization in the nearby graphic. We don't have direct access to this reservoir as we do to our conscious memories, but it's part of our legacy as humans and resides within our psyches, overlaying and interacting with our consciousness. Its contents affect us in subtle ways, and it's an important part of our ethical intelligence. As this book unfolds, you'll see its power and appreciate its significance as you make personal and professional ethical judgments.

Next, and closely related to the idea of the human collective unconscious, is the primal relationship.

The Primal Relationship. The Primal Relationship is the elemental, unique and special connection we humans have to one another—an invisible but real link. In this book, I talk a lot about connections and interconnections. This connection is special, which is why I've italicized it throughout the book. The Primal Relationship is the pristine prototype of all relationships. It's important because it's where our ethical intelligence manifests in the real world. Our ethical intelligence lives in our consciousness but shows itself and grows within the Primal Relationship, its soil. Flowing from the Primal Relationship is our millennia-long struggle for our individuality, our Selfhood.

Our Struggle for Selfhood. It happened at Runnymede, England, on June 15, 1215. King John signed the Magna Carta, the first-ever written description of the individual human rights we all now assume are justly ours—security of property, equality before the law, habeas corpus, regular fair elections, freedom of speech, jury trials and the inviolability of contracts, just to name a few. Given the wide expanse of time humans have occupied this planet, human individuality, or the Self, is a relatively new idea. In the beginning, there was no me, only us. Emerging and differentiating the Self from the Other has been and is an ongoing struggle.

I ask you to consider these terms and foundational ideas and keep them in the back of your mind. Together they form the foundation for your ethical intelligence.

INTRODUCTION

Sitting in a Phoenix hotel room late the night before my second doctoral residency was to begin in May 2006, I was deciding on the research topic for my doctoral dissertation. I was scheduled to present my proposal to a committee of faculty and fellow doctoral students early the next morning. (Yes, sometimes my work is just in time. Please don't tell my students!)

As I sat there pondering what to research, the term "ethical intelligence" flashed through my mind. My ever-present guardian angel told me that was my topic. I dutifully Googled the term and, among the 300 hits that came up, found very few references that didn't involve spying and espionage. Essentially, there was almost nothing written about the subject.

The subject of unethical behavior among business executives was something that had intrigued me my entire business career. So I quickly assembled a PowerPoint presentation, which I enthusiastically unveiled to my committee the next morning.

The response was less than optimal—well, perhaps, "Are you insane?" would be a better description. I was given all the standard reasons why it was a terrible idea. "The subject is too broad. There is little prior research to build upon. It will take far too long. We already know why these things happen—they're all a bunch of greedy bastards! The subject is way too complex. You're never going to get CEOs to talk to you about such delicate matters. Finding a dissertation chair could take years."

Well, they were right on that last point. It took over a year and a half to find someone brave enough to chair my dissertation committee.

That Doubting Thomas meeting began a quest that ended with the publication of my dissertation on ethical intelligence in 2012. During those six years, I combed through 45 centuries of ethical intelligence literature (more than 9,000 works). I garnered exclusive interviews with CEOs and other C-Suite executives from the Fortune 1000 (more than a year of outreach), and I analyzed a massive amount of data.

This project sows the seeds of a new millennium of ethical intelligence thought, research, education and practice. It's a millennium within which ethical intelligence—an ancient legacy and the birthright of human beings—will again come to infuse human conduct, soothing and healing the aching wounds of conflict.

> **As a reminder, the following two chapters are taken from (My Book), *Ethical Intelligence: The Foundation of Leadership*. The word "book" used in the following two chapters refers to My Book. Likewise, the word "chapter" used in the following two chapters refers to chapters in My Book.**
>
> **My Book is available on Amazon in hardcopy and eBook formats at www.ethicsbook.com, or www.ethicalintelligence.com.**

CHAPTER 1

CULTURE—A FORCE FIERCE AS FIRE

> You control ethical behavior with culture.
> Culture is everything.
>
> *Fortune 1000 CEO*

It's early on a summer morning, and a semi-retired chief executive is sitting on his back deck enjoying a freshly made cup of Kenyan coffee. His yard guy is manicuring a wondrous garden-like back yard. The birds are singing, and the mountain peaks in the distance are lit up by the sun. Sam, who holds a doctorate in engineering, is talking about the importance of organizational culture in controlling ethical behavior. He's finally put down his iPhone, to which he's been glued. And to illustrate his point, he relates a story of a young straight-arrow West Point graduate, hired to work a trading desk.

The story unfolded when, earlier in his career, Sam was running a high-pressure, high-stakes financial instrument hedge fund. Sam was a quantitative guy, a "quant," competing in a cutthroat take-no-prisoners industry where a trading desk could make or lose millions in a matter of hours. So whatever "edge" a trader could establish translated into extraordinarily high returns. Everyone pursued any "edge" available. Sam worked hard to keep his firm legal and ethical within that high-pressure milieu, but the anything-goes industry culture made it a constant challenge. He began his story:

"We hired a 38-year old guy as a trader for our bond desk. We always told people when we hired them, don't bring your Rolodex. We don't want you to bring any information. If there is any doubt, don't use any knowledge that might be proprietary to your former job. Secondly, we encouraged people when they joined us to make sure they had done whatever they had to do—including we'd give them time off to go back—to close out tasks and projects so that they had left their previous employer on a good note wherever possible.

"After [the new trading guy] had been there a couple of weeks, he stopped in my office one Friday afternoon and told me he was not going to be in on Monday because he had to take care of some business for his previous employer. I said, 'Okay. When will you be back?' He said, 'I'm not sure. I'm being indicted by the grand jury on Monday.' So I said, 'Well, maybe we ought to talk about this.'"

At this point, I asked Sam what he was thinking as this young man's story was unfolding. Taking a sip of coffee, Sam thought for a moment. Then he said, "My heart was greatly saddened. The industry and that band of crooks he worked for ruined his life." With a more solemn face, Sam continued his story.

"So my CFO and I sat and talked to this young man. The CFO asked him what happened. The young man said, 'We never gave kickbacks. What would happen is we would bid on a deal, and if we won the bid, we would return a small portion of our profits as a thank you to the guy on the other side of the deal for doing business with us. Because, in that business, it was all word of mouth and there was no advertising, we would just share the advertising dollars we would have otherwise spent. It was never quid pro quo. It was never you give us the deal, and we give you the dollars. It was just—if we were awarded the deal, a small portion of our profits on that deal would go back to the other counterparty rep.'

"So our CFO, being more astute about this than I was, asked, 'How big were these numbers? What kind of dollars are we talking about?' This 38-year-old young man said, 'It would never be over *$200,000 a month.*' Now, remember, this was a Boy Scout, a graduate of West Point, a commander, a strong Christian with a strong ethical foundation—but he was sitting in an organizational culture where the company had created these myths and its rationale for doing things.

"He had been immersed in it, and he had just sort of bought into the party line and never really thought about it. He was sincere in our meeting. He was just as sincere as it is possible for a human being to be—he believed that there was nothing wrong with this, even though a typical counterparty rep would have earned about $400,000 per year. He was convinced it was not a quid pro quo."

Hidden Hand of Culture

The young trader in Sam's story had lost his connection to the realities of the outside world because of the toxic cultural pool in which he swam every day. I imagine that young trader walked through the door of his former employer with his West Point values intact—honor, integrity, truthfulness and service. But unbeknownst to him, his subconscious mind was absorbing the hidden corrupting particles of the organization's culture. He was like a fish swimming in polluted water.

The philosopher and economist Adam Smith gave us the idea of the "invisible hand" of economics: pursuing your own self-interest serves the greater good of the economy and society. In the case of the hidden hand of culture, the greater good is served when there is a healthy and righteous culture. The opposite case is also possible, as we see in the story of the young trader. He marinated every day in an organizational cultural stew in which an obvious case of bribery became something virtuous and "just the way we do things around here." Culture will change you or you can change it, and you'd better know the difference.

> Culture will change you or you can change it, and you'd better know the difference.

Knowing the difference, however, is not easy. We can objectively evaluate the young trader's story, mystified at how he missed it, because we have perspective. We have objective benchmarks that inform our judgment. But when you're sitting in a distorted environment day after day, that setting steals your perspective. You begin to see the world not as those outside the situation would see it, but only from the distorted point of view from within. We often want to believe that what we feel in our gut is not real. We want something so badly we override the flashing red lights, the alarm bells and the knot in our gut. This is exactly what happened in our next story.

The CEO who related this story began his career in finance. Tom earned his MBA from a prestigious school and passed the CPA exam right after graduating. He was on the fast track to success, moving up rapidly in his career. Tom became CFO of a publicly traded company before the age of 30. He prided himself on his ability to read people and situations, but he succumbed to the kind of cultural seduction that happens to all of us.

"Early in my career, there was an international organization that I really wanted to work for. It had a stellar reputation and hired only the best and brightest. The recruiting process was very selective, arduous and included a daylong assessment with a psychiatrist. The company was growing rapidly, and landing a job there often meant receiving valuable stock options.

"I was thrilled to get an offer and to begin working there. After a couple of months on the job, however, I realized, from the inside, the company looked more like a criminal cartel than a business. We lied to everyone—and we were proud of it. There were highly valued stories of how we had fooled the auditors time and time again. I remember one story in particular that still stands out in my mind. We'd signed a deal to construct a factory in a foreign country. Unfortunately, the ship containing all of the equipment for the factory sank in a bad storm. Instead of writing off the investment, we kept it on the books and lied to the auditors whenever they questioned the investment's value.

"There was a legendary story of how we flew a team of auditors to the site of the factory in a helicopter. Of course, the site was overgrown with the tall grass and vegetation of the kind you would expect in a jungle. Our team had given the auditors waist-high boots and machetes, suggesting that we could land in a clearing and let them hike to the factory that was nestled in some trees, which is why it couldn't be seen from the air. Our team mentioned to the auditors that the place was infested with poisonous snakes and several other types of threatening wildlife. After thinking it over, the auditors decided that a close-up look was unnecessary."

This story seemed so incredible to me, I interrupted Tom with a question. I asked him how in the world a Big Eight (now Big Four) CPA firm could be so easily duped. He said, "They wanted our business. We were an up-and-coming client, and in the grand scheme of things, that one transaction wasn't a big deal."

Tom continued, "There were many other 'stories' that were a part of this company's culture. All of these stories were touted as highly successful episodes of deceit, and these very smart and highly accomplished professionals saw nothing unusual about this. One day, I went home and my wife mentioned to me how working for this company was changing me. She said, 'When you first started telling me these stories from work, they made you uncomfortable. Now you seem unconcerned and accepting even though what the company is doing hasn't changed. I don't like the changes I'm seeing in you.'

"That's when I knew I had to leave. It was a hard decision to make because I had only been there six months, and that's not something you want on your resume, especially with the excellent reputation this company had. It took a while, but I found a better job. Within a year, my previous employer had filed bankruptcy and was in the midst of an SEC investigation. Eventually, several of the executives went to prison, and the people who still worked there had their personal and professional reputations tarnished forever."

Like our young trader, this CEO had allowed the culture to seep into his subconscious without noticing it. He had slowly acclimated to an organizational culture that at first seemed incompatible with what he knew was right. This can happen to anyone. We enter into a situation thinking we know what is right, but over time, we are swayed by peer influence, especially if we believe those peers are smart, well-educated, know more than we do and are on the fast track to success.

This also is especially true if it's something we really want. Our emotions subtly kick in, and we rationalize. We make excuses. We override our instincts. Over time, our denial dulls our instincts, and what we once knew was unacceptable slowly becomes just the way things are. Fortunately for Tom, he had someone from outside the organization's culture—his wife—holding him accountable to an external reality.

If organizational culture has such hidden, seductive and effective powers, how do we define it?

Cultural Gestalt

The power and influence of organizational culture on behavior can't be overstated. Organizational culture is a force as fierce as fire. A controlled fire is a force of creation. It can conquer, calm and create. An uncontrolled fire is a force of destruction. It can damage, disrupt and destroy. Organizational culture is an all-consuming force. When controlled, it will create an environment within which ethical conduct and R^2 Behavior flourish. When neglected and uncontrolled, it will create an environment within which the survival of the fittest devours all within its path, including the C-Suite and board of directors.

I use the term cultural gestalt because culture is more than simply the sum of its parts. Organizational culture is multiplication, not addition. It's a set of values, stated and otherwise. It's a collection of myths. Organizational culture is a mystique created by a founder, a set of traditions people hold dear. It's a dress code one dare not violate, it reflects the CEO's behavior, it's a force that gets into our collective unconscious. Organizational culture controls you without you even noticing.

> Culture is more than simply the sum of its parts. Culture is multiplication, not addition.

Many years ago, I was privileged to be part of the Price Waterhouse accounting and consulting organization, now PricewaterhouseCoopers (PwC). At the time I was there, PwC had a company dress code that was strictly enforced. Men wore dark suits, white shirts and subdued ties. Women wore dresses or professional pantsuits, a modicum of makeup and very little jewelry. Even though that was decades ago, that dress code has stuck with me. Recently I attended a business meeting wearing my dark suit, white shirt and subdued tie. Other attendees, who were dressed more casually, chided me for "ruining" the dress code. My retort was, "I can't help it. I was raised at PwC."

> The men at Price Waterhouse wore starched underwear, but the men at Lybrand Coopers wore no underwear at all.

Organizational culture controls you without you noticing, even decades later. When Price Waterhouse and Lybrand Coopers were merging, there was much talk about the clashing cultures. The standing joke at that time was that the men at Price Waterhouse wore starched underwear, but the men at Lybrand Coopers wore no underwear at all.

Because the CEOs of both firms understood the hidden hand of culture, they spent years successfully merging the two dissimilar cultures. These two CEOs instinctively knew that organizational cultural gestalt was more than the sum of its parts. They also knew you have to pay attention to the parts because they can either help or hinder your drive to create the organizational culture you want. So let's examine four of the most commonly cited elements of culture: values, myths, artifacts and tradition.

Values. Values are ephemeral things. They have no physical being, but we see their manifestation in the things people and organizations do. I discuss values and principles throughout this book because they loomed large in the stories I heard from C-Suite executives. In this instance, we are talking about organizational values as opposed to personal values. And make no mistake, these two sets of values are different and not always aligned.

Many organizational cultures have split personalities between their stated values and the values that actually prevail within the culture. This creates a condition I call *cultural hypocrisy*. It's a lot more prevalent than most C-Suite executives might care to acknowledge. We've all seen organizational values statements prominently featured on posters, computer screensavers and internal corporate bling such as coffee mugs. Typically, such statements might say:

- *We value integrity.*
- *We value fair dealing.*
- *We value truthfulness.*
- *We value respect.*
- *We value accountability.*
- *We value hard work.*

When these values statements are aligned with actions taken by all members of an organization, we say the culture is healthy and R^2. A COO of a Fortune 300 company described it this way:

> "In this company, if you're not highly ethical—and I would add to a great extent moral—you're not going to move up in the company. One of the things we say is, 'We hire and fire to our core values.' I can think of several situations where we let people go who were good performers, very strong performers, because they missed it from an ethical standpoint. You can't work here if you don't live by our number one core value—doing the right thing every single time regardless of what you believe are the consequences."

The question is, can personal values be at variance with organizational values? Does it matter how one of your team members treats their spouse or children? Is it important that your CFO cheats a little bit every time she plays golf? In Chapter 11, we'll talk about this issue in greater depth, and I will introduce a tool—Heart-Mind Maps—to disclose personal and organizational value misalignments. This next story emphasizes the importance of that misalignment.

I was gratified to be sitting in Gwen's expansive 40th-floor office overlooking the skyline of one of the world's largest cities. She earned an engineering degree when most women didn't pursue such an education. Gwen began her career on the bottom rung of the ladder wearing a hard hat, boots and coveralls. She had more than a passing familiarity with dirt, debris and danger. Gwen fought her way to success in a world once solely dominated by men. Now she is a Fortune 400 Chief Administrative Officer. Given her educational background and practical mindset, there's little gray in her understanding of values and the difference between right and wrong. She described the importance of values in her organization, as follows.

"You've got to do the right thing. You have to lead by example. You have to embrace the culture of the company, which for us, our values and vision are at the top. You have to always stay true to that. And if you don't have it from the top… so you see that poster over there [points to a poster containing company values]…I've been in different leadership situations through my whole career when sometimes it was a poster. And sometimes it was really, really pushed as being a foundation. And not that the people that had it more as a poster didn't believe it, they may have. But you can't just put it on a poster.

"A guide that we use is, if you are thinking about a decision and you question that decision, think about it in perspective of if it would be on the front page of the Wall Street Journal…and you were reading about the decision you made, how would you feel seeing that? How would you feel with your family reading about that decision that you made? And, if you are the least bit uncomfortable, you are probably making the wrong decision. So, that's how we continue to reinforce it [pointing to the poster on the wall]."

Gwen went on to describe something unique within their organizational culture:

"I think every once in a while, you have people making bad decisions because they are worried about what might happen if they made a mistake and they're trying to cover it up. But, again, lying, cheating…it's not the right thing to do. Hopefully, we have a nice balance. Like for us, we use mistakes, if there wasn't any bad intent, as a learning opportunity. That's part of our culture. I think it all works, but

I think leaders need to be mindful of the fact that they can't pressure people to not make mistakes. And encourage them to learn from it because if people are worried about losing their livelihood because they made a mistake...maybe they'll lie or try to cover something up."

If we closely examine Gwen's last paragraph, we see a value that's not listed on the organization's values statement. Her organization allows people to learn from their mistakes. Although this value doesn't appear on any "official" organizational literature, it's well understood within the culture. The important takeaway here is that values statements are good, but values behavior—R^2 Behaviors—are better and have a much more profound effect on organizational culture. Why?

> Values statements are good, but values behaviors—R^2 Behaviors—are better and have a much more profound effect on organizational culture.

The answer is simple—actions speak louder than words. Living your values is more important and effective than listing and talking about them. And more important still, we get more of what we reward. If we want our organizational culture to reflect our values, we must reward values behaviors that are consistent with our values statements. When we don't, we get cultural hypocrisy.

Myths. Organizational mythology is another element of organizational culture, and often it's the product of values behavior as opposed to values posters.

The dictionary tells us that a myth is a traditional or legendary story—with or without basis in fact—usually of a heroic or notable deed. All organizational cultures have myths. Some are true, some are true but highly embellished, others are completely false but conveniently fit into a preferred narrative.

Whether true or not, myths are a powerful foundation upon which organizational cultures are built. The young bond trader we met in Sam's story acted upon his organization's cultural myth: We don't advertise. Therefore, we share a "small" portion of our profits with those individuals who give us business—and it's never been considered a bribe!

Here are two real examples of "myth" creation.

This first story was related to me by Gordon, an up-and-coming youngish CEO running a Fortune 500 international pharmaceutical company. Confidential and proprietary information in that industry is the lifeblood of competitors' market positions. This is especially true of new drug development pipelines. One day, a treasure trove of competitive information about a major competitor made its way into Gordon's organization. What he did is the sort of thing from which myths are born.

> "We recently received an email containing some very highly confidential information by mistake. When it came to light, I made sure few people saw it, other than those who had already seen it. Then we sent it back. Organizationally ... it shocked a lot of people. Many of our research folks really wanted to see that information. It got out pretty quick that we had it. It was information about a competitor, and we were able to keep it contained. No copies were made, and it was sent back with the appropriate level of disclaimer. Some people might call that stupid, but I called it the right thing to do.
>
> "So, I just think it's hard to pinpoint ... that golden moment when you have to make a critical decision ... like the confidential information. It would have been nice to be able to read through that stuff, but the reality was, if the employees saw me doing that, then how could I ever argue that it

wasn't the right thing to do? If I would've done the wrong thing, I'm sure the next time something similar happened, I wouldn't have seen it. It made me feel like we have the right values as an organization."

This organization has thousands of employees. The story will be remembered and repeated. Over time, the details of the story will change, be embellished and take on a much more heroic tone. But the essential message of the myth—that we do the right thing here even when the wrong thing would have been to our advantage—will remain intact.

The second story, related to me by Randy, a Fortune 500 COO, may also be a heroic tale, but it has a different ending. It also created a myth with very different overtones—well, I'll let you decide. This story took place early in Randy's career, when he and several other members of the company's leadership team accompanied the CEO on a trip to Africa in an effort to close an elusive but crucial deal with a particular tribal chief.

"Early in my career ... I was probably in my early thirties and just married... our entire leadership team and our CEO went to Africa to close the largest and most important deal our company had ever proposed. We were trying to get exclusive mineral rights and a contract to build a major refinery. We had been negotiating with this particular tribal chief or warlord, with sketchy results. Our people on the ground told our CEO the only way we could close the deal is if he personally came and dealt directly with this chief.

"The CEO insisted that all of us accompany him—must've been eight or nine of us—as a show of respect and honor. We got there and spent four days in hard negotiations and finally agreed on a contract. As a sign of his gratitude, the chief threw this sumptuous party and celebration the last night we were there. It was quite an event. The chief pulled out all the stops. The event was held on the shores of this beautiful lake with flowing white sand. We had big bonfires, all kinds of food, unlimited adult beverages and native dancing girls.

"After everyone had eaten, carried on and participated in many toasts, some of the chief's men erected a tent a ways down the beach. The chief brought out a—shall we say 'attractive,' if you know what I mean—young woman and introduced her to our CEO as one of his most prized wives. The chief stopped the music and very publicly presented the woman to our CEO as a show of friendship and great respect for our new venture together. The chief explained that it was a tradition with his people on such occasions for chiefs to exchange valuable gifts, at which time he sent the young woman off to the tent to spend the night with our CEO."

At this point in the story, we were both laughing so hard, we took a short breather. I asked Randy if this "gift" was unexpected, or if anyone had even thought about the local culture before the celebration. He said he didn't know, but for the rest of his career, he made sure someone did! He continued.

"Our CEO began feverishly explaining to the chief that he was unable to partake of such a wonderful gift for 'manly' reasons related to a 'war' injury. But he did offer one of us in his stead. Suddenly, we're looking at each another like deer in the headlights. We were speechless. It was kind of like watching your career pass before your eyes in slow motion. We knew someone was going to have to step forward. There were only two guys on our team who weren't married—Jerry and Nelson. After what seemed like an eternity, Nelson stepped forward and said he would be delighted to honor the chief's 'gift.'"

As you can imagine, Nelson's willingness to do what it took for the team's success became legendary. His level of "sacrifice" eventually became a litmus test within the organization. It became "the way we do things here," and Nelson marked the path to the top. Eventually, Nelson became CEO, and he is now regarded as a senior statesman in the industry. As I said at the beginning of the story, I'll let you decide about this particular myth, whose origins were grounded in a true story.

As time passes, myths like these accumulate and solidify into an organizational cultural mythology that forms a strand of the DNA of an organization's cultural gestalt. One myth was about always doing the right thing. The other myth was about doing whatever is necessary for the team's success.

Artifacts. An artifact is a monument or a remembrance. It is a physical manifestation of an important event or myth. Artifacts are important because they remind those who weren't there of the significance of whatever the artifact symbolizes. The Washington Monument in our nation's capital is a reminder of the greatness of our first president. It symbolizes his dedication to the values underlying our nation's founding. Artifacts serve the same purpose within organizational cultures.

For example, it's common for an underwriter to provide the CEO of an IPO client a Deal Lucite containing a replica of the cover of the firm's S-1 Registration Statement. I was once privileged to have the inventor of voicemail serving on one of my Boards of Directors (yes, he was frequently chided for the "monster" he had invented). His company maintained a framed copy of the original voicemail patent as a cultural artifact.

Sometimes an artifact is a major public and decisive act, as related by the following CEO. Tom is a burly take-charge kind of a guy—some might say he's impulsive. He doesn't suffer fools well, and he doesn't like hearing excuses.

> "I jumped on a plane and went to New York along with a couple of my key direct reports. We did an on-site investigation with our internal audit staff for about three or four hours. We did some interviewing, and we fired the entire department. It was difficult to do. It was the right thing to do. The employees had decided that if they couldn't get signatures on contracts, they would be in trouble. So they decided to forge customers' signatures. We started getting calls from customers who wanted to know why their service was continuing. In a concerted effort to get ahead of this, we immediately began contacting customers. We alerted them about the forged contracts. At the end of the day, we were successful in retaining a lot of the business because we acted."

> *We did an on-site investigation. We did some interviewing, and we fired the entire department. It was difficult to do. It was the right thing to do.*

In that organization, this act is memorialized as the "massacre in New York." It has informed and affected the organization's culture to this very day because of its suddenness and finality. The "massacre" enshrined the CEO's passion for taking action—as in "we don't talk; we act." The "massacre" also set the standard for doing the right thing even when it hurts.

A final element of the organizational culture gestalt is tradition.

Tradition. Merriam-Webster's dictionary defines tradition as "an inherited, established or customary pattern of thought, action or behavior." Most of us understand traditions and the power they can have on behavior. For example, Thanksgiving is not only a holiday but also a long-standing tradition in the United States, and the Thanksgiving turkey is the entrée of choice.

Several years ago, my wife and I went to an extended family member's home for the holiday. After arriving, we sensed there was an unusual level of consternation because the host was serving ham instead of turkey. Traditions have a powerful effect on our behavior, and in most cultures, deviations from traditions are not welcomed.

> Traditions have a powerful effect on our behavior, and in most cultures, deviations from traditions are not welcomed.

Organizational cultural traditions are very similar. For example, part of the Avon organizational culture is the annual Avon Walk for Cancer held in cities across the United States. This is a cultural tradition that raises millions of dollars for cancer research, and it exhibits the three important elements of any tradition: shared identity, unique ritual and a remembrance of past triumphs. This organizational cultural tradition is a win-win for all participants. It adds value to the Avon brand, and it brings together cancer survivors and their family members as they generate valuable research funding.

An organizational cultural tradition can also be a long-term loser. Earlier in my career, I worked for a major auto manufacturer that we'll call Acme Motor Company. Acme's founder was a firm believer in the company's "self-sufficiency"—some called it paranoia. Over the years this belief morphed into the tradition that if something didn't originate at Acme, it wasn't important enough to consider adopting. This tradition was called "the Acme way," and it stifled innovation and enshrined obsolete practices within the organization's culture. In the long run, "the Acme way" nearly bankrupted the company.

Culture Dysfunctions

We've all heard the term "dysfunction" as applied to social groups, families, teams and bureaucracies, just to name a few. Webster's dictionary defines dysfunction as "a consequence of a social practice or behavior pattern that undermines the stability of a social system." In other words, something is not working correctly or is simply malfunctioning. From my research, I've identified six organizational culture dysfunctions, which I call the Sick Six:

> Organizational culture dysfunctions are like termites, silently eating away at the foundations and structures of organizations.

- *Organizational hypocrisy*
- *Wet work*
- *Omerta*
- *Arrogance, hubris and entitlement*
- *Pressure to perform*
- *Shoot the messenger*

These dysfunctions are like termites, silently eating away at the foundations and structures of organizations. Left unchecked, these destructive pests will reduce even the largest and most powerful organizations to skeletal shells, unable to withstand even the slightest breeze of adversity. When the Sick Six are silently at work in your organization, you have jumped the shark without repellant or Kevlar wetsuit. It will be bloody. Just hope the blood's not yours.

Hypocrisy. Organizational hypocrisy is defined as establishing desired standards of behavior but then rewarding behavior that deviates from those standards. Hypocrisy is one of the most destructive and toxic dysfunctions. Like a weak acid, it slowly erodes shared values.

Jack grew his career under such conditions. He is a former COO of a Fortune 100 firm. Jack has lived and worked in some of the toughest and most undesirable places on earth. His language often runs to the "salty," and he had this to say about organizational hypocrisy:

"Companies have stated missions, visions and ways of doing business. But in actual operations and in the running of the business, those are not rewarded. People are smart. If the company says you ought to do this, this and this—ethically and for safety reasons—but the guys who get promoted are those who just get things done no matter what, they break all the ethical rules. Then the culture fails. It generates an undercurrent and an underculture. And that underculture becomes a wink-and-nod of how to get ahead no matter what's said.

> "When you look down [the ladder], people are smiling at you. And when you look up, you're seeing a different view. The point, is the only way up the ladder is to be an asshole."

"The bad thing is that, over decades, those people get to be CEOs. And those CEOs got there by looking up the ladder and smiling and doing what's expected—not what's written. Of course, when you look up the ladder, there is a queue, and when you look down the ladder there is a queue. When you look down, people are smiling at you. And when you look up, you're seeing a different view. The point is, the only way up the ladder is to be an asshole. Once you have that in place, culturally, deviant behavior takes decades to change out."

The condition that Jack is describing is every manager and leader's worst nightmare. Unfortunately, all too many managers and leaders are clueless about how quickly even a little organizational hypocrisy spreads. Or they're fearful about the short-term effects on operating results if they take a principled stand.

I once consulted with a business services organization where Lamont was the star sales performer. Lamont sold ten times as much business as anyone else. Because of that, he was not only allowed to break whatever rules he liked but was handsomely rewarded for it. Senior leadership looked the other way because they were afraid of losing the business Lamont was generating. It was widely known throughout the organization that Lamont was "bulletproof," or that "no one screws with Lamont." Slowly but surely, Lamont's bad behavior metastasized throughout the sales organization. Organizational hypocrisy is a lot like cancer—you can't tolerate or contain just a little of it.

Then, one day, the organization received a subpoena from the U.S. attorney's office. The U.S. attorney was investigating allegations of bribery and other illegal activities involving certain members of the sales staff's dealings with federal contracting officers. You might be surprised to learn that Lamont was not involved. Lamont's transgressions ran more toward sexually harassing female colleagues. He was very good at selling, so bribery was unnecessary. But many of Lamont's colleagues needed an extra edge because they weren't endowed with Lamont's selling prowess.

As a result, some of Lamont's colleagues engaged in questionable activities they *thought* were countenanced by senior leadership. Lamont's colleagues believed the only thing that mattered was the end result. After all, Lamont had been sexually harassing female colleagues for years, and it was always "handled." This is frequently the result of a wink-and-nod culture. You can't have one set of stated values but reward a different set of values behavior. If you do, it invariably leads to what I've called organizational wet work.

Wet Work. Organizational wet work is doing what *you believe is expected*—not what's written in the company's code of conduct—and then *not mentioning it to anyone*. I have adopted this term from the world of spies and espionage. In that world, "wet work" is a euphemism for assassination. But the term has the added connotation of giving plausible deniability to your superior. This means you understand the hidden content of a superior's message even if that content is unspoken or unwritten. So, if you're caught, your superior can deny having had any foreknowledge of your activities.

> You understand the hidden content of a superior's message even if that content is unspoken or unwritten.

In some cases, this can be a benign aspect of an organization's culture, but in most cases it's not. Life is messy. It serves up dilemmas that don't conveniently fit into a formula or get resolved using a rulebook.

Here is a case related by Derek, a senior executive whose career included stints as a country manager and drillship captain, discussing some of his work overseas. You judge whether this case is benign or something more serious.

"We have to realize that, over a couple hundred years in the United States, our ethics and jurisprudence have evolved to a point where we don't tolerate baksheesh payments or lagniappe considerations. In other parts of the world, this is not only tolerated but part of the culture. And, in fact, recompense is based upon this understanding.

"The question becomes then, what does the country manager do when he has a motor in customs, and it's going to take a couple hundred dollars U.S. to get it out today? And if that doesn't happen, it's going to stay in there for another week, and the company's going to lose a half million dollars. But that's okay. I can handle it with my expense account. I can say it's just the cost of doing business. And when you think about that as a concept, and it just takes a couple hundred dollars, you can hide that amount in your expense account, and nobody says a word. Or you don't even report it on your expense account. You just think of it as the cost of doing business, and you're getting plenty of money for doing it.

"But what happens if the customs guy says, 'I need $300,000?' And if the country manager pays it, he still saves the company a million dollars in shutdown time for a week. What does he do? What does the company do? Our lawyer would say, 'Look, if you're faced with this $300,000 question, you've got to call the legal department.' And then the country manager says, 'Well, we've got a local contractor that can take care of this for us, and no one will ever be the wiser.' Then the lawyer says, 'You can't tell me that!'"

> The country manager says, "Well, we've got a local contractor that can take care of this ... [$300K 'gratuity']." Then the lawyer says, "You can't tell me that!"

This is a typical and straightforward case of organizational wet work. The official company policy is, "We don't pay bribes of any size and for any reason." But the work still needs to be done at the lowest possible cost. So the company may decide that paying a $300,000 gratuity to save $1 million is a logical trade-off if it can be done quietly and under the radar.

Using a third-party local vendor, in this case, would be a convenient way of accomplishing that objective. The local vendor makes the payment, which is most likely not illegal in that country, and increases his invoice to the company by the $300,000. Except for a small group of individuals who all have something to gain by remaining silent, no one ever knows the difference. If the payment is ever discovered, senior management can rightly claim they had no knowledge and certainly didn't approve of the payment. Everyone wins! Or not—I'll let you decide.

Here is a much more subtle case of organizational wet work as related by Mark, the CEO of a Fortune 1000 multinational distribution company. Mark described himself as someone who "lives his life pretty straight ahead." He attended parochial schools and had a fond memory of Sister Mary, who "kept everybody on the straight and narrow." He described a wet work situation where the company had recently missed its numbers and was punished by Wall Street with a sharp stock price decline.

> If someone's got to be held accountable, and if it's *you*, you've got to step up to it.

"Situations surface all the time. If certain things come down that are not good, people will try to pass the buck. I think someone's got to be held accountable, and if it's you, you've got to step up to it. That's the ethical thing to do.

"Recently, we had a situation where we missed our numbers, and everybody was blaming everyone else. I said, first of all, I am the CEO. I am responsible. So I could've been pointing my fingers, and I certainly had plenty of places to point. I expect people to be accountable.

"There's tremendous pressure [to hit Wall Street expectations], and I think there was a desire on my people's part to come up with a forecast that they thought was acceptable to me. I do think, looking back on it, I may have been a little bit too aggressive with my expectations, and maybe people weren't as objective as they might otherwise have been in preparing the forecast. So we took an unnecessary hit."

Mark's story is a more refined case of organizational wet work because there was no illegal or unethical activity involved. Mark had been aggressive in describing his intention to reach a certain quarterly "number." He didn't overtly tell his staff to overstate the forecast. Such a statement wasn't needed. His staff "understood" what was necessary, and they obliged. Then Mark had to deal with the aftermath.

Having spent a large portion of my professional career in accounting and finance, I am all too familiar with this organizational cultural dysfunction. In one organization, every quarter we'd get the "number" we had to hit. Upon receipt of the "number," we'd work our accounting magic, figuring out a way to reach it without going to jail, and everyone would be happy. We all knew what was expected, and it was *never the subject of conversation*, which leads to our next cultural dysfunction, organizational omerta.

> In many organizations, speaking the unspeakable, no matter how true, is a career ending event.

Organizational Omerta. Organizational omerta is a code of silence, an organizational silence that often accompanies organizational wet work. I have borrowed this term from the world of organized crime, in which violating the code of silence is often a death sentence. This may seem like a harsh characterization, but in many organizations, speaking the unspeakable, no matter how true, is a career ending event, as this senior leader clearly articulated.

> "[A code of silence] is an inherent belief that has been supported over a culture inside the organization for years. If an employee stands up and says, 'This is unethical, I'm not going to do it,' they are viewed as someone who doesn't understand the corporate goals and what should be considered a gray area. Hence, they're not fit for their position. They [the employee] have taken a position that will be difficult for the corporation to explain, and they should have chosen not to bring the subject up. It should have been resolved *without anyone knowing about it.*"

Recent allegations about the Veterans Administration (VA) serve as an example of organizational omerta. A senior medical director of the VA informed senior VA leadership about a serious backlog of veterans awaiting treatment. Instead of recognizing the problem and working on a solution, senior VA officials drummed the concerned medical director out of the organization and found other "team players" who subsequently engaged in a multiyear cover-up, which allegedly caused the deaths of numerous sick veterans.

Here are short comments that provide further examples. The first is from a Fortune 1000 COO describing his initial experience as an operating executive.

> "The first time, I ran a P&L. And after my first year, I was having a conversation with my vice president, and I said, 'I've

learned three lessons from my first year here.' And she said, 'What are they?'

"I said 'One, pad your budget by 20% because it's going to get cut. Two, spend as much capital money as I can regardless of my budget until you tell me to stop because that's what everybody else does. And three, don't raise my prices so I can grow my business until you start screaming at me for margins.' She laughed and said, 'You're a piece of work!'

"Now, I never did those things. But those literally were undertones in that business that were the unspoken truths."

We also have this CEO's recollection of working in a foreign environment where executive kidnapping was a common occurrence:

"I worked for a major company where we had one of our executives kidnapped in a foreign country. No one ever talked about it. But one of the guys out of our internal security group, who once worked for the FBI, showed up with a briefcase. The briefcase changed hands, and the executive was freed. And nobody talked about it."

At this point, you might be asking yourself what's the big deal with these situations? It makes sense that you'd pay a ransom for a valuable executive and hope that no one heard about it. And padding your budget is something everybody does.

But a cow can't be a little pregnant. She's either pregnant or not. An organization either has a code of silence or it doesn't. Organizational members either engage in activities they can discuss freely, or they don't engage in those activities. The VA enforced a code of silence, and we now understand the aftermath.

An organizational code of silence is often accompanied and enabled by the toxic triangle of arrogance, hubris and entitlement.

Toxic Triangle: Arrogance, Hubris and Entitlement. Most organizations have some level of arrogance, hubris and entitlement. Market leaders, especially, may expect to earn the highest margins because they have the "best" in their industry segment. This triangle of egotistical attitudes becomes toxic when it so infects an organization's culture that everyone within the culture actually believes what they say about themselves and the organization. This is one of the poisons that killed Enron.

The following Fortune 100 CEO was keenly aware of this toxic triangle as he described an incident within his organization.

> Hal is one of the most senior executives I interviewed. He's led some very large organizations with far-flung operations. In this story, one of his direct reports, Bill, the COO, had hired his son to run a significant part of the company's business. Because Bill's son didn't report directly to Bill, the company's anti-nepotism policy was waived. Hal had learned, via an "unofficial" company grapevine he nurtured, that Bill's married son was having an affair with a married woman who worked in his organization. The affair wasn't completely "undercover" and was causing problems because certain staffers were getting "favors" and "special treatment." Arrogance and hubris in action aren't pretty. Here's what Hal had to say.

> "People think that because they're in the C-Suite, things should be swept under the doormat."

> "People think that because they're in the C-Suite, as in this case, things should be swept under the doormat. Or they believe matters can be treated differently than if you're handling somebody

several rungs down the ladder. I've seen it before. I've even had people that know me think that these things [ethical problems] can be just managed away. They'll propose, 'Let's relocate the individual. Let's put them into a different department.'

"Usually those things don't work anyway. The reality is I think they [lower level employees] lose respect for the organization. And I think it causes a loss of trust in the leadership of the organization. I think it tends to bring a number of other things into question, especially if it's prevalent in the company."

In the end, Hal saw to it that Bill's son realized his career aspirations would be more successfully fulfilled in a different organization, and he left the company.

Remember Sam, whose story about the young bond trader opened this chapter? He offered these incisive comments about the toxic triangle.

"As you move up in an organization, as you get increasingly more responsibility, the temptations toward hubris get bigger, and they frequently get more subtle. As the chairman and CEO, it's easy for me to justify an action because I do have an obligation to the shareholders. Any guy who's smart enough to be a CEO is smart enough to figure out a way to rationalize anything he wants to do. You tell me whatever you want to do, and I can rationalize why that's good for the shareholders."

I'll let Terri, one of the few women I was privileged to interview for this book, end our discussion of the toxic triangle. This subject was of particular interest to her because she had never considered herself arrogant, full of hubris or entitled to anything. She had to fight her way through the glass ceiling to reach the C-Suite of her health care organization. Nothing had ever been just handed to her. But in the end—well, I'll let her explain.

> "Your driver picks you up at your front door. When you arrive at your office, everyone is attentive to you. Anything you want is quickly provided. Staff even begins to anticipate what you'll need or want, and it appears magically on your desk or conference room table. When the company jet is not available, you always fly business first class, with all arrangements made to the smallest detail. Once the plane is off the ground, you find your staff has already ordered your drinks, selected your wine and ordered your favorite meal. After years of this kind of treatment, you're tempted to think of yourself as royalty.
>
> "Once that kind of thinking creeps in, you're really in trouble because royalty can do anything they want without adverse consequences. They simply decree it, and it happens. If you're able to do that, and you do, you lose your ethical moorings. Your moral compass becomes unhinged from reality. And, because you're surrounded by people whose job it is to please you, you rarely get pushback from clearly unethical acts."

These moral lapses often manifest as an unhealthy organizational pressure to perform, regardless of the costs.

Pressure to Perform. We all feel a pressure to perform at our best, and for most of us, this pressure comes from within. Pressure to perform in this context, however, refers to the overwhelming and relentless 24/7/365 pressure to meet short-term organizational goals that often override the stated organizational core values or the code of conduct. For example, meeting Wall Street's expectation for this quarter's earnings or not missing periodic creditor-imposed debt covenants. One CEO described his constant struggle with the unrelenting pressure this way:

> "Well, I think it's just the short-term nature of the demands for results *every* quarter. Quarterly earnings, and now we have Wall Street analysts forecasting our earnings to the *penny* ... a one-penny shortfall and your stock price tanks five to ten percent, and it's not even our forecast. So I think the endless short-term quarterly demand for results. Sometimes I think, 'Man, if I do [the right thing] it will trash the quarter.'
>
> "The right answer isn't always obvious when you're under pressure. A lot of money is involved, you're personally financially at risk, you're strung out financially and you're trying to make some stock option number. Or other pressures are weighing on the situation, like keeping your job. Your thinking can get really cloudy."

> "A lot of money is involved, you are personally financially at risk, you're strung out financially and you're trying to make some stock option number."

As you're reading this, I know your heart really bleeds for this guy. He's making well into seven figures, lives in a beautiful home with a well-manicured lawn, has access to a chauffeured limousine and flies on the company jet. That may all be true. But do you really want someone who's running a company in which you have invested your money living in constant fear? Remember, in Chapter 1 we showed how fear of loss is one of the most powerful of all human motivators. This type of fear almost always leads to irrational judgments. Ethically intelligent organizations don't motivate people this way.

Stan was one of the most experienced and well-seasoned CFOs I interviewed for this book. He is a CPA and has an MBA from one of the top business schools in the country. In his three-decade career, Stan has seen just about everything. He and I have much in common, especially when it comes to the unbearable pressure to "make a number." He talked about a scary experience he had early in his career.

"About 25 years ago, I was working for a private equity fund. The fund had borrowed about $250 million from a 'Mideast oil sheik,' if you know what I mean. It was for a big marina real estate project on the West Coast. The project was maybe 85% done, but out of money. And we had to ask the 'Mideast oil sheik' for more money to finish the project. I was sent in to help get the funding and save the project.

> "My CEO said, 'Just increase the sales price.' And, 'I said I can't do that. I'm out here every day, and we can't even sell them at the current price.'"

"So the project CEO said, 'Let's put together a sales forecast showing how we'll sell off the condos and the boat slips. That will cover everything and make everybody happy.' I did that, and I discovered we were short $30 to $40 million from where we currently were, much less the additional money we needed to fund the project. The project CEO said, 'That's easy, just increase the sales price to a level that will close the funding gap.' And, I said 'I can't do that. I'm out here every day, and we can't even sell the condos at the current price, much less a fictitious higher price just to hit a number.' I didn't know what to do.

"I knew a guy who was the chief executive officer of a similar management firm. This was a guy who really knew how to run the business. I went to him. He was kind of a mentor, and he said, 'Don't ever cross that line.' He said 'Once you cross it, it gets easier to cross it again.' So he said, 'The first thing is be upfront about it. If you hide it, then you hide the second thing, and the third thing and the fourth thing.'

"So, I learned early in my career just to be upfront about it. Let the chips fall where they may. You'll never regret it, and you won't have to keep looking over your shoulder. So, now that's the model I always follow. I went back to the project CEO, and I gave him a letter that said 'I will not present these numbers, and if you force me, I'll resign. I won't do it. I can't do it. And here's why. We're asking people for more money based on false projections, and it's just not the right thing to do. Let's just tell them the truth. The project may be screwed, but it will be a hell of a lot more screwed if we don't get the money. Or, we get the money under false pretenses, which is even worse.'"

> "I will not present these numbers, and if you force me, I will resign. I won't do it. I can't do it."

We all live with stress. As managers and leaders, we're expected to live with it and produce results. If we can't, perhaps we're in the wrong line of work. Unfortunately, this is the prevailing attitude in many organizations today. I'm asking us to think differently. We can produce the same or better results with a better approach. In today's world, too many organizations use fear as the chief motivator: fear of loss, fear of shame or fear of failure. It doesn't have to be this way. In Chapter 11, we'll pick up this subject again, and I'll lay out a better way.

Once organizational culture is infected with the pressure-to-perform toxin, it invariably leads to our final cultural dysfunction: shoot the messenger.

Shoot the Messenger. The shoot the messenger dysfunction is an organizational practice that outwardly encourages truthfulness and "whistle blowing" but, in practice, secretly punishes such behavior. This cultural perversion forms a barrier to truthful information flow—something managers and leaders desperately need—and indirectly encourages unethical behavior. Stan, our senior CFO, offered this observation about shooting the messenger and the resulting fear injected into the organizational culture.

> "What I see is a lot people who are—especially in the financial world—just scared. They're scared of getting yelled at. They're afraid they might get punished. I run into financial people who would rather hide under their desk—they would rather cover things up—then tell somebody that they made a mistake when they prepared their budget, or that the operating results are actually that bad. Instead, [some will say] 'I'll cook the books. Hope things get better and cover it up.' Or, instead, 'I'll move these numbers around a little bit, and, hopefully in a month or two, things will get better, and I'll be able to fix it.' Then, the problem instead of reversing itself gets bigger. So, to disclose the bigger problem, they would have had to disclose how they covered up the smaller problem. So they bury themselves deeper and deeper."

I hope you're beginning to see a pattern in the stories. These organizational cultural dysfunctions—organizational termites—

create an undercurrent of fear. People who are motivated by fear often make deadly judgment calls. Think back to the airline crash we discussed in Chapter 1. Almost 600 people lost their lives because of one person's fear-based judgment. Ethically intelligent organizations don't function this way.

Gerald is another CEO who started his career in accounting and finance. In addition to his "day" job, Gerald mentors up-and-coming leaders not only in his organization but also through various charitable outreach initiatives. We talked in his office, which was somewhat cramped due to overflowing floor-to-ceiling bookcases. Gerald's story is unique because it demonstrates how a fear-based culture can jump from a single organization into an entire industry.

> "Earlier in my career, I was CFO of a Fortune 500 organization. One of our subsidiaries was a military contractor that had been underperforming for several years. Our board decided it was time to change out the subsidiary's leadership team. My CEO and I arrived at the subsidiary's offices early one Tuesday morning. Our plan was that my CEO would interview and discharge the subsidiary's president, and I would interview and discharge the subsidiary's controller and CFO. After informing the controller that he was being terminated, he asked me how we had found out about their secret overbilling scheme. I was shocked to hear his spontaneous admission of perpetrating a fraud [double billing on several military contracts]. As the controller talked, I recorded several pages of notes detailing the overbilling fraud.
>
> "Later on during lunch, I relayed the story to my CEO, a retired army general. The CEO advised me that [the controller's allegations] were probably just the ranting of a dis-

gruntled employee and to forget the entire matter. He further advised me to 'shred' my notes and to proceed as if nothing had happened in my meeting with the controller.

"Later that day as we were flying home, I began to worry about the bind I was in. Following the CEO's order was unethical and illegal. If I followed his order, I'd violate my professional ethics and open myself up to prosecution for covering up a crime and obstructing justice. But on the other hand, if I didn't follow the CEO's direct order, I would be fired. He didn't tolerate any hint of insubordination.

"After much anguish, I turned the information over to our outside legal counsel. Our outside legal counsel forwarded the information to the appropriate governmental officials, and eventually both the subsidiary's president and controller were sentenced to prison. Ironically, my CEO and our organization received a 'good citizen award' from the military for turning ourselves in. Within a year of the convictions, however, I was dismissed. My CEO, who was quite influential in our industry, made sure the word got out that I was not 'team player.' I never worked in that industry again."

> "[The CEO] further advised me to 'shred' my notes and to proceed as if nothing had happened in my meeting with the controller."

> "My CEO, who was quite influential in our industry, made sure the word got out that I was not a 'team player.' I never worked in that industry again."

Destroying someone's ability to make a living working in a particular industry sends a powerful signal. It's a pernicious strategy for enforcing not only an organizational code of silence but also industry-wide omerta. It enables organizational and industry wet work, which is how we get deadly mine explosions and chemical spills. This is how seemingly rock solid organizations like Enron collapse in a single day. It's how a financial stalwart like Bear Stearns threatened the entire financial system. Organizational termites are deadly.

Most of these cultural dysfunctions are not singular occurrences. They occur as pairs or even triangles. The effects are synergistic. Organizational wet work rarely happens by itself. It requires organizational omerta to succeed. Organizational omerta is enforced with shoot the messenger. We know that arrogance, hubris and entitlement occur as a toxic triangle. The effects of these dysfunctions are multiplication, not addition, which is why I've called this the cultural gestalt. Once these dysfunctions are embedded, they're extremely difficult—but not impossible—to change.

A Success Story

Can toxic cultures be rescued? Yes, but once the fire of a toxic culture is out of control and consuming everything in its path, stopping its advance takes strong actions. Tough measures are required to turn around an out-of-control organizational culture. Illustrating that difficulty, a COO related the following experience.

> "The only force to change unethical behavior is leadership that doesn't promote those who are ethically questionable. Fire a few people. Leadership has to make examples. People have to make it known that this is not just bullshit we're talking

"The only force to change unethical behavior is leadership that does not promote those who are ethically questionable. Fire a few people."

because we have to please Wall Street. The tough thing about that is now and again you're going to have to fire somebody who has delivered really good business results. I went through some of this back in the early 1990s. I delivered tremendously good business results. But the company said, 'You're broken; we're going to fix you.' It was a big investment by the company. The company also said, 'You're going to have individual coaching. We're going to coach you for 24 months. But if you don't pass this program, you're fired.'"

This executive was "fixed," but the personal cost was high. He had to unlearn much of what had led to his prior success. The industry in which his company competed had succumbed to organizational termites. His company was cleaning out its termites, but the industry was yet unchanged, and he was required to produce the same operating results without resorting to well-known "shortcuts" that his competitors still used. During his two-year reeducation program, he and his organization paid a heavy price. But in the end, they emerged more respected and one of the preferred providers in their market space.

In my research, I heard several success stories in which CEOs made gut-wrenching decisions and restored ethically intelligent organizational cultures. Here is one of those stories. As with all the stories I've presented in this book, I have changed many details to ensure the anonymity of the storytellers. In this case, the company competed in an industry with odious marketing practices. I have selected the electronics industry as a stand-in for the real industry. If you work in the electronics industry, please don't be offended.

The CEO in this case has a reputation as a standup guy, and for good reason. He is well known, and many of his colleagues were surprised when he accepted the challenge of turning this organization around, particularly given its industry. But turn it around he did. And in so doing, he showed the way forward. He demonstrated the possibility of cultural redemption and changed the way an industry operated.

From Strip Clubs and Ladies of the Evening to Family Outings.

"One of the toughest issues I faced is when I became CEO of an electronics components business. This was a tough business, and the people who were in it—and the rules of the game—were such that a large part of the business was done in men's strip clubs and sometimes involved procuring prostitutes—and in some extreme instances exchanging things like cocaine or other illegal substances. It was the existing culture. We had products that we had to market, so we needed to do what was necessary to compete.

> "The rules of the game were such that a large part of the business was done in men's strip clubs and sometimes involved procuring prostitutes."

"The ethical dilemma was obvious. So we made a policy decision, and it was implemented though our culture, which was: We don't entertain customers in men's clubs. And we don't engage in or fund immoral behavior. But we recognized the rules in this business were very loose. When we would hire a new marketing rep that was coming from one of our competitors that did [strip club marketing], we would sit down before we hired them and explain that we don't do this. We explained that we wouldn't pay expense reports from places like Vera's Cabaret, Lucy's Love Palace or similar establishments. First of all, that practice self-selects. You begin hiring people who don't really believe in Vera's Cabaret or Lucy's Love Palace. But you have to provide an alternative that works.

"So we struggled with this for a couple of years. We got together what I called an Advisor's Council. And to be on the Council you had to be active in your church. And it involved hourly workers in the warehouse. It involved the support staff members who were active in their church. We took people from all levels of the company. It wasn't just the management. I would present these issues to the Council. It was a group that varied from about 8 to 12 members over the years. I presented this particular problem to them.

"The alternative the Advisor's Council came up with was that instead of doing business in men's clubs, we're going to do business with the customer's family in a family-friendly way. So instead of spending $400 at Vera's or Lucy's to take Mr. Smith to the men's club, the alternative was we're going to send an airline ticket to Mr. Smith's wife and invite her to visit with him. So the rule was you send the ticket to Mr. Smith's wife, and you and your wife or girlfriend can take Mr. and Mrs. Smith to anywhere *Mrs. Smith wants to go*. If she wants to go to the men's strip club, you can go there, and we'll reimburse you. If she wants to go to the opera, you'd better learn to like opera.

> "If she wants to go to the men's strip club, you can go there, and we'll reimburse you. If she wants to go to the opera, you'd better learn to like opera."

"So that's the solution—you can't just say no. You can't just say we're not going to do business in men's clubs. You have to replace it with a different philosophy. In this case, it was we're going to be the smartest and hardest working guys, and we're going to have an alternative social venue that we control—our culture will reflect our core values."

This strategy was extremely successful. Customers' wives eventually heard about what this CEO's company was doing and demanded their husbands begin buying from them. The CEO ended up changing industry practices. But don't think it was easy. This transformation took many years and a lot of hard decisions. For a period, the organization experienced a high turnover rate. And many in the industry thought this CEO was fighting a losing battle and would eventually fail. Changing a dysfunctional organizational culture is heavy lifting. Creating and nurturing an ethically intelligent organization is easier and smarter.

One of the most senior CEOs who participated in the research for this book had these well-chosen words of wisdom about organizational culture:

> "I will tell you without any reservations ... there are very few things I am absolutely certain about ...very few. But one of the things I am absolutely certain about is that you control ethics/morality in any organization with culture. The culture is about who you are and how you do business. And you don't do it with statements ... those silly little things you hang on the wall ... those motivational posters. You do it every single day by conscious example and parables."

This chapter about cultural fire is one of the longest in this book, and for good reason. Organizational culture is the foundation upon which ethically intelligent organizations are built. Unless you've created a solid foundation, everything else, while important, is secondary. It's like building a house on a weak, unsteady and shaky foundation. The walls, the roof, the interior fixtures, can be of impeccable quality. But if the foundation isn't right, all of the other quality is wasted.

It's hard to execute an exquisite strategy when the windows won't open and the doors won't close.

I end this chapter with a quote about organizational culture from Peter Drucker: "Culture eats strategy for breakfast." Culture is like a fierce fire. It can create or consume. As a leader or manager, you have no choice but to pay attention to culture. Ignore it at your peril because it will burn you every time.

> You have no choice but to pay attention to culture. Ignore it at your peril because it will burn you every time.

Chapter Highlights

- Organizational culture is a gestalt. It's a set of values, stated and otherwise, a collection of myths, mystique created by a founder, a set of traditions people hold dear, a reflection of the CEO's behavior, a force that gets into our collective unconscious.
- Culture will change you, or you can change it, and you'd better know the difference.
- Organizational culture is multiplication, not addition.
- Organizational culture is the foundation upon which ethically intelligent organizations are built.
- Culture is like a fierce fire. It can create or consume.
- It's much easier to heat a room with a controlled fire in a fireplace than to extinguish a blaze that's destroying the building.
- Values statements are good, but values behaviors are better and have a much more profound effect on organizational culture.
- Organizational cultures are destroyed by dysfunctions (termites), which are the Sick Six—hypocrisy, wet work, omerta, toxic triangle, pressure to perform and shoot the messenger.

- Exercise constant vigilance and, if you see termites, call the exterminator.

Questions for You

- Are you okay with your CFO cheating on the golf course on Sunday and signing your SEC filings on Monday?
- Who or what outside of your organization holds you accountable?
- Can you list some of the key traditions in your organizational culture?
- Do you have any organizational termites? How do you know?
- Are there any unspoken truths in your organization? Do you know what they are? How do you find out?
- Can you describe your organizational culture in a single sentence?
- When was the last time you had a cultural audit?
- Do your team members engage in wet work? Do you know? How do you find out? If they do, would you like to know what they're doing?

CHAPTER 2

ETHICALLY INTELLIGENT ORGANIZATIONS

An ounce of prevention is worth a pound of cure.

Benjamin Franklin

Buzz ... buzz ... buzz ... buzz. The vibrating phone on the night stand finally stirred Jim from a deep sleep. He reached over and grabbed the phone to see who was calling at this hour of the night. It was Fred Carrington, the head of his board's audit committee. Jim answered the phone.

"Hi, Fred. This must really be important for you to call me at this time of night."

Fred responded in a somber tone of voice Jim has rarely heard. "Jim, sorry to wake you up. I hope I didn't also wake Cara."

Jim glanced over at his wife, who was sleeping peacefully. He said, "Not a problem. Cara could sleep thorough a rock concert. What's so important that you're up at this time of night? Your tone of voice tells me it's not good news."

"I just got off the phone with Roger Pinkett, the audit partner in charge of our audit this year. Roger is a college fraternity brother, and he gave me a courtesy heads up call a few minutes ago. We're going to receive an interim internal control report tomorrow implicating our Mystic Controls operation in a substantial accounting fraud."

Jim was accustomed to receiving bad news, but accounting fraud—not on his watch!

"How high does it go?" Jim asked.

"You're not going to want to hear this," Fred said, "but all the way to the top."

"So, is Kurt involved?"

"Roger tells me that Kurt is the moving force behind the fraud," Fred said. "And it gets worse. Kurt has been siphoning money through a number of front companies in order to pay gambling debts and support his mistress."

"That miserable bastard!" Jim's outcry woke Cara.

"Jim, what is it?" Cara turned on the bedside light and saw tears trickling down her husband's cheeks.

"How much theft are we talking about?" Jim asked.

"At least $20 million," Fred said, "maybe a lot more. You're not going to like this, either. There is also evidence of money laundering on behalf of some very bad actors. It seems Kurt's mistress has some close ties to the drug trade. Jim, I'm sorry to bring you this news at this hour. But I figured a heads up was better than a bolt out of the blue in the morning. We'll talk more tomorrow."

> "You're not going to like this either. There is also evidence of money laundering on behalf of some very bad actors."

Jim ended the conversation and sat in silence for several minutes.

"Jim, you're scaring me," Cara said. "What is going on?"

"Our little girl and our two granddaughters are about to pass through a very long valley of sorrows," he said. "I should never have allowed her to marry Kurt. There was always something about him ..."

This story eventually ended with long prison sentences, hundreds of millions of lost shareholder value, many business and professional reputations tarnished and a shattered family. Suppose we could prevent these types of scandals? Or, if not prevent, at least maintain a heightened awareness of high risk managers and leaders?

Lock the Barn Door

Let's stop locking the barn door after the horse is gone. We must end our reactionary response to ethical failures like this one. We have an eight-decade-long history of *responding and reacting* to ethical scandals, beginning with the passage of the enabling legislation for the Securities Exchange Commission in 1934 and 1935. Since that watershed moment, we've added hundreds of federal and state laws, and thousands of federal and state regulations, and we've sentenced thousands of managers and leaders to prison. Yet we've hardly made any progress in preventing the problem because every time we close one fraudulent door, another unforeseen and unexpected door opens. There's a better way.

As I've previously mentioned, this book is the product of a research project that began in the spring of 2006. During the years since then, I've assembled a large and growing body of actionable knowledge, some of it presented in this book. The research technology I used for this book is applicable to the real world. Using that technology, I can produce Heart-Mind Maps for organizations and individuals. These maps show the influencers behind ethical judgments—a glimpse into hearts and minds. They show us what's going on when that person is in the Sweatbox. Why is this useful?

> Yet we've hardly made any progress in preventing the problem because every time we close one fraudulent door, another unforeseen and unexpected door opens. There's a better way.

Heart-Mind Maps are useful because they show us what's going on behind the scenes when someone is making an ethical judgment. For example, a Heart-Mind Map would show us whether an executive was motivated more by fear or the organizational culture when resolving ethical dilemmas. Most organizations would prefer the organization's culture as the prime driver behind ethical conduct. How might this work? Here are some sample maps taken from my research data. As we review these illustrations, please keep in mind that, although I've chosen pie charts as a presentation format, this data can be presented in any number of ways.

Also, this technology is still in its infancy. There is much more to learn about how to reliably generate, interpret and *ethically* use these Heart-Mind Maps. This sample, however, provides a glimpse into the promise of this hermeneutic-phenomenological technology—prevention and/or interdiction rather than post-mortem horrified reactions, regret and remonstration. Here is our illustration.

XYZ CORPORATION'S HEART-MIND MAP

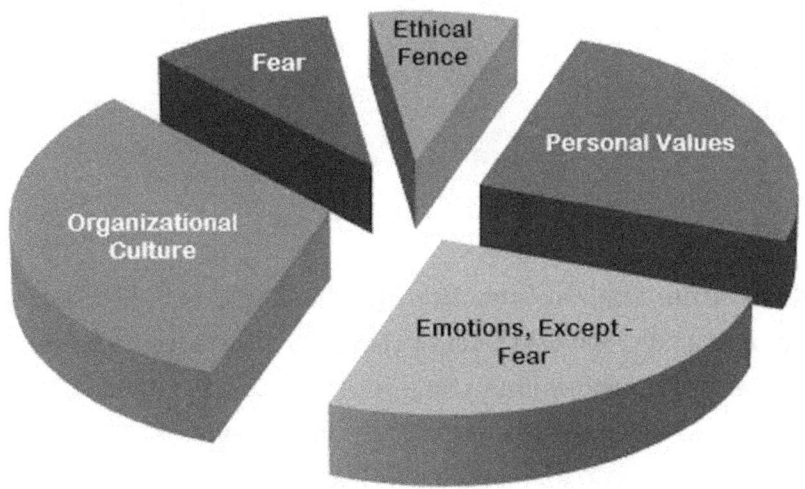

XYZ CEO HEART-MIND MAP

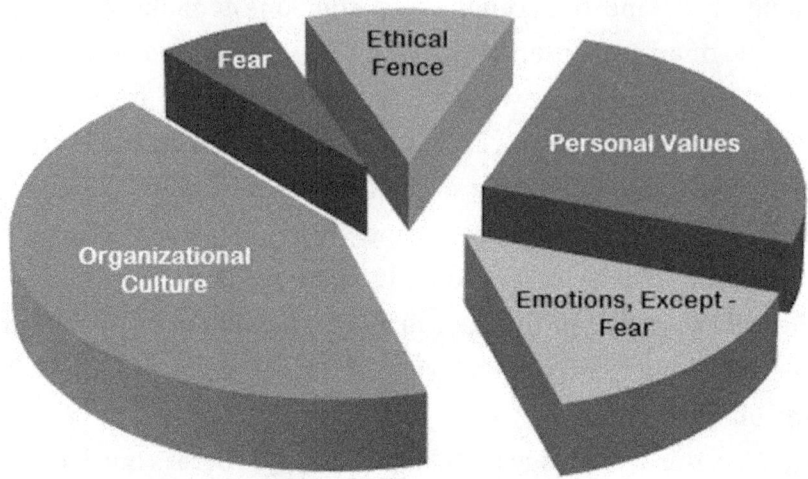

XYZ CFO HEART-MIND MAP

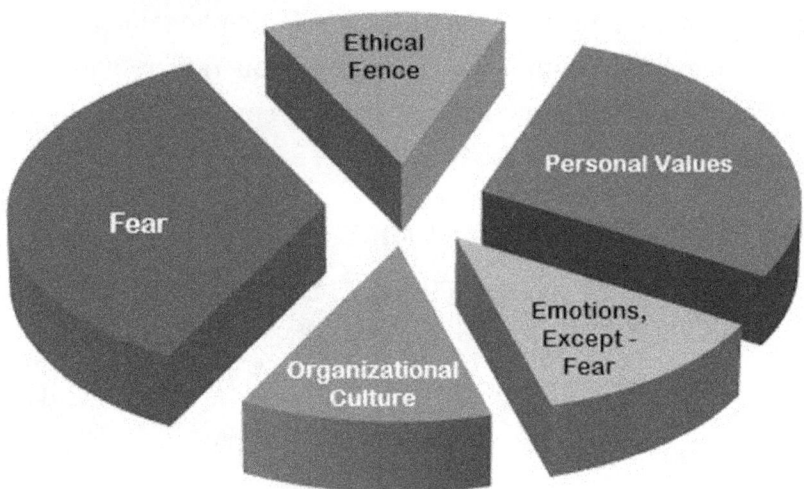

Illustration Explanation. Although the data is real, XYZ Corporation is a mythical organization. Here we have three Heart-Mind Maps—XYZ Corporation's composite, the CEO's individual map and the CFO's individual map. The composite map is a consolidated view of XYZ's 21 individual Heart-Mind maps, which I created by merging all 21 maps into a single view. Each map shows the type and weight of ethical judging influencers present in the Sweatbox during ethical judging.

What it Means. Heart-Mind Maps convert the ephemeral and subjective into a form more easily grasped and understood. These Heart-Mind Maps incorporate the theory and real-world experience I've discussed in this book into something concrete. If we look at the composite Heart-Mind Map, as an example, we see that more than a third of the influencers are emotions. We can also note that the personal and the organizational cultural influencers are about equal. If you look at all three Heart-Mind Maps, it's noteworthy that the Ethical Fence and comfort zone are approximately equal in all three maps.

> Heart-Mind Maps convert the ephemeral and subjective into a form more easily grasped and understood.

Now let's take a look at some interesting comparisons. The CEO's Heart-Mind Map shows a reduced influence of emotions during his or her ethical judging. We also note that the personal values take a back seat to organizational culture in this executive's ethical judging. This tells me that the CEO is a bit calmer and cooler during ethical judging than the organization as a whole.

If we now consider the CFO's Heart-Mind Map, we see a much different story, which is not surprising given the public company CFO's professional balancing act.

In this case, we see that nearly half of the ethical judging influencers are emotional, with fear a notable standout. It's significant how organizational culture plays a much diminished role in the CFO's ethical judging as compared to the CEO, meaning this CFO may be less of a "team player" than his or her contemporaries. Having been a CFO of a public company, the composition of the CFO's Heart-Mind Map is not surprising. In this case, we can see that personal values and emotions represent nearly 70% of the influencing factors in this executive's ethical judging.

Let's dive into this dilemma a bit more deeply.

In a public company, the CFO serves two masters—the company and its stakeholders *and* the public in the person of regulators—regulators who can put you behind bars. Although the Sarbanes-Oxley Act of 2003 equalized CEO and CFO liability in cases of fraud, regulators routinely view the CFO as the police officer on the beat, especially if the CFO is also a licensed professional, such as a CPA.

In many public companies, the CFO comes under significant pressure from the remainder of the C-Suite team to "hit" the right number every quarter. As a result, CFOs are often less influenced by organizational culture and rely more on their Internal Compass, Ethical Fence and ethical comfort zone when in the Sweatbox. This CFO's Heart-Mind Map illustrates that real-world experience. If we were to look at the Heart-Mind Map of the Chief Compliance Officer, we might find similar results.

Let's consider a slightly different scenario.

These days, we have diverse multicultural organizations. These organizations can have members with very different worldviews. We've seen the profound effect worldview has on an individual's Internal Compass. Suppose we find a senior executive within an organization whose individual Heart-Mind Map reveals that his or her Internal Compass plays a much larger role in ethical judging than the organization's culture. In such a case, we might conclude that such an executive, when in the throes of the Sweatbox, is more likely to make ethical judgments contrary to the organization's culture. Do we work to change his or her worldview? If so, where do we go with this powerful tool?

Moving Forward. As is usually the case, new tools and technology are often two-edged swords. Such tools and technology can do much good but also, when used inappropriately, can cause great harm. I think, in the case of this technology and tool, it's appropriate to invoke the Hippocratic oath: First, do no harm. There is still much to learn about using this new technology. In our Ethical Intelligence Research Center, we're continuing and expanding that research. As we move forward, we can make great strides in understanding and interdicting unethical behavior. It's my pledge that this new tool and the underlying technology will be used for good and not harm.

> I think, in the case of this technology and tool, it's appropriate to invoke the Hippocratic oath: First, do no harm.

Roadmap To An Ethically Intelligent Organization

In the previous chapter, I presented a detailed Roadmap to an ethically intelligent life. Here, I'm presenting a Roadmap to an ethically intelligent *organization*. There are some similarities but mainly differences between the two Roadmaps. Although organizations are living creatures (organism is the root word for organizations), they are very different from human beings. As a result, our Roadmap reflects that dissimilarity. It's more generic and lacks the specificity of the human Roadmap.

The ethically intelligent organization Roadmap possesses all of the organizational lessons presented here, but those lessons must be tailored to fit each organization. Here are the general organizational lessons of the Roadmap to an ethically intelligent organization.

1. **Truth**
2. **People**
3. **Right-Thinking-Right-Acting (R^2 Behavior)**
4. **Acting**
5. **Culture**
6. **Cloister**
7. **Otherness**

Before we start working through these organizational lessons, I want you to know there are resources available to help you. The Boardroom Partners (www.boardroompartners.com) website contains an array of resources available to help you work through this journey. And, of course, we're available for consultations.

As we discuss these organizational lessons, please keep in mind that these are not stand-alone unrelated lessons. They are intrinsically intertwined, symbiotic and synergistic. For example, creating a right-thinking-right-acting (R^2) organization is dependent upon truth-telling. The more truth-telling that occurs within an organization, the easier it becomes for people to consistently do the right thing, which contributes to the organization's R^2 Culture.

Now, let's get started. Here are the seven organizational lessons.

> Lying is an insidious poison to any organizational culture. It corrodes the very essence of trust.

Truth. As I've said before: Stop lying! Creating an ethically intelligent organization begins at the same place that awakening an ethically intelligent human life begins—telling the truth. Truth-telling is *the* essential foundation for not only creating an ethically intelligent organization but any organization that effectively fulfills its purpose.

Lying is an insidious poison to any organizational culture. It corrodes the very essence of trust. Lying corrupts decision-making, and it promotes a perverse Darwinian culture where the fittest liar survives. Lying organizations seldom succeed.

I've seen these effects firsthand. As an auditor, employee, officer and consultant, I've worked in and observed hundreds of organizations and their respective cultures. Organizations that tolerate lying underperform those that don't. I've seen some organizations where lying was considered a high art form, and people were praised for creatively deceitful skills. Every one of those organizations eventually failed, some in spectacular public implosions. Why is this important?

It's simple: lying steals freedom. I've made this point once before, and I emphasize it again because most people don't understand this aspect of lying. Lying steals your freedom to choose right actions. Let's consider a simple example.

Many organizations tolerate so-called "budget padding," which is a common form of organizational deceit. Managers and leaders justify this practice because forecasting is imprecise, and budget overruns can be costly to your career. So they add a little "fudge" factor that will enable them to either hit or come in a little under budget, something that always looks good. At the micro level, this may seem shrewd and acceptable.

At the senior leadership level, however, this is a potential disaster. Let's say that there are three levels of consolidation contained within the forecast. If each of those levels added even a 6% padding factor, the padded consolidated budget would be 18% higher than a truthful budget. That 18% difference could be a decisive factor in not launching a new product. Or it might influence the choice of health insurance provider with expanded benefits. Because of the 18% difference, senior leadership would be deprived of positive project selection. As a senior manager or leader, it means you've lost an element of your freedom to correctly choose.

Lying is anathema to creating an ethically intelligent organization. Managers and leaders should demand the truth, tell the truth to others and themselves, and live a life based on truth. One of the best ways of accomplishing this goal is to hire the right people.

> Organizations are created by and for people. Organizations contain people. Organizations reflect the people who populate them.

People. Hire and nurture ethically intelligent people. I know this seems obvious, but it's impeccable advice. Organizations are created by and for people. Organizations contain people. Organizations reflect the people who populate them. If someone is not ethically intelligent when they walk through your front door (and most won't be), make sure you provide a welcoming environment that supports them on their journey to an ethically intelligent life.

There is an important symbiosis and synergy neatly interlaced into this second organizational lesson. Organizational members self-select in or out of organizations. Once you've set the organization on its ethically intelligent growth journey, every ethically intelligent person who comes on board increases the incentive for those who are not ethically intelligent (or on the journey) either to begin their journey or leave the organization. This creates a virtuous self-reinforcing loop. Your job as a manager or leader is to get it started and nurture its growth. You give it life and love until others join you. Success is in multiplication, not addition!

Ethically intelligent organizations are places where telling the truth is the number one value. Members of ethically intelligent organizations don't lie, don't tolerate those who lie and respectfully admonish those who do. Such organizations don't mislead customers, even when it's more profitable to do so. They shoot straight with their employees. Such organizations admit mistakes when they occur, take responsibility for those mistakes and equitably compensate anyone damaged from such mistakes. These are the organizations that create an R^2 Culture and have a bright future.

R^2 Behavior. Create a culture of R^2 Behavior or an R^2 Culture. We defined R^2 Behavior as right-thinking-right-acting behavior. It's an expression that aptly describes a virtuous practice, colloquially called "doing the right thing." We know from our discussion in Chapter 5 that R^2 Behavior is timeless and has three parts: truthfulness, discernment and integrity. We also know that most managers and leaders want to lead a team of R^2 people executing a vision and a mission within an R^2 organization. How do we get there?

We've already covered the first two steps. An R^2 Culture is grounded in truthfulness. As I mentioned previously, in all of my interviews with senior business leaders, telling the truth was always considered the right thing to do. That's step one.

Hiring ethically intelligent people is step two. People who do what's right in all circumstances are the backbone of an R^2 organization.

> People who do what's right in all circumstances are the backbone of an R^2 organization.

Steps three and four are a bit more challenging to describe—a discerning organization acting with integrity. Crafting a discerning organization acting with integrity requires not only hiring discerning people possessing integrity but also an organizational structure whose decision-making and judging processes are intrinsically discerning and reflect integrity. I know this sounds a bit complicated and esoteric because we're ascribing human characteristics to something that isn't human. It's both possible and necessary, however, to create an R^2 organization with these characteristics. Let's consider an example that will help illustrate my point.

Most business organizations have internal decision-making and judging processes designed to maximize profit and the return on investment to shareholders. There is nothing wrong with this orientation. Let's consider a plant manager who is deciding on modernizing certain aspects of the plant's manufacturing infrastructure. The modernization would add years of competitive productivity to the plant. The existing internal decision-making process is driven by the plant's projected discounted cash flow. In addition, the plant manager's annual bonus is tied to the plant's profitability.

On the surface, this decision-making process seems straightforward. We project the additional future cash flows of the plant after the improvements and decide if those improvements result in an appropriate return on our shareholders' investment. There is, however, an internal conflict in this process. Investing in the current year reduces not only the plant's profitability and cash flows but also the plant manager's bonus. Our non-discerning internal process is challenging our plant manager's integrity because the right thing to do is make the investment this year. As someone who has been compensated under this kind of arrangement, I can tell you that today's bonus is much more important than next year's. I might not be around next year!

How do we fix this? We change the process to make it more discerning of the inherent contexts. We allow the plant manager to share in future projected results even if the plant manager is not around to see future results. This incentivizes decision-makers to do the right thing which, in this case, is to do what's appropriate for the long-term health of the organization and return on investment to its shareholders.

This is a simple example, but it demonstrates how organizations sabotage themselves internally with non-discerning decision-making and judging processes. Discerning organizations acting with integrity don't have these internal conflicts. Organizational members should see R^2 Behavior as the force that animates the organization. They will see it only if organizational managers and leaders act well.

> Great managers and leaders are great actors. They show us. They lift us with their example. They inspire us with actions. They walk the talk.

Acting. Great managers and leaders are great actors. They show us. They lift us with their example. They inspire us with actions. They walk the talk. My pastor says we act out more sermons than anyone will ever preach.

The application of this wisdom is universal. Faith-based pursuits is just one arena of success. Without right actions, your words are empty, producing scant outcomes. Great managers and leaders are great actors. The rest of us, not so much. This is one of the few leadership skills that I strongly advise you to work on. If you're not an effective actor, you won't be an effective manager or leader. Acting skills are important for managers and leaders, but they're not a substitute for sincerity. I'm not suggesting that you acquire acting skills so that you can feign false concerns and an artificial attitude. Whatever you do as a manager or leader must come from an internal sincerity. Otherwise, you'll become known as a fake or a phony. Let me offer a few examples.

Many years ago when I was offered my first "formal" leadership assignment, my manager taught me what I'm teaching you.

I was having a difficult time leading my team. I didn't have the respect of my team members, and they were not receptive to my leadership. My team was in chaos. I went to my manager for advice. He told me what I'm telling you. I was not acting like a leader. My actions were tentative, and I showed that I was unsure of what I was doing. My response was, "That's all true. I'm *not* sure I know what I'm doing. I'm afraid of making mistakes, especially in front of my team members."

His response was, "Fake it 'til you make it." That advice rings in my ears to this day.

Here's another example. I was once mentoring a young aspiring professor. After several weeks spent in the classroom, she came to me and said teaching in a physical classroom wasn't for her. She was going to concentrate on teaching only online. Knowing how bright and capable she was, I asked her why she was entertaining such a foolish notion. What she told me is instructive. "I feel so inadequate when I'm standing in front of the class. Many of the students are more experienced and older than I am. When they ask me a question that I don't know the answer to, I freeze and look foolish. In an online environment, the students can't see me. So I have time to research the question and provide an answer. I never look like I'm not in control."

I told her what I'm telling you. When you're asked a question to which you don't know the answer—and this can happen frequently in a technical and evolving subject like accounting—act like you know the answer and think logically. Use the question as a teaching opportunity and solicit responses from the other class members. They may know the answer, and you may learn something. And there is nothing wrong with saying you don't know the answer off the top of your head, but you surely know where to find it. Act the role until you *are* the role.

There are many other examples I could offer. Think back to Chapter 6 and our discussion of Dr. Martin Luther King, Jr., when he first became leader of the bus boycott group. He didn't want the job. He was scared to death of it. But he stepped up and acted like a leader until he became one. There is nothing deceptive or underhanded about acting. Acting is a noble profession. Combine it with excellent leadership skills, and it can move mountains. Embed this idea into your organizational culture.

Culture. Culture is a force as fierce as fire. Harness the fire. Culture is to an organization as emotions are to individual humans. Emotions are the energy of life. They provide the passion for great achievements.

> Culture is the life force that animates organizations. It transforms ephemeral missions and vision into reality.

Culture is the life force that animates organizations. It transforms ephemeral missions and vision into reality. Culture is the conduit for transfusing ethical intelligence into your organization. Cultural transfusion permeates and infuses your organization just like an injection fills a living organism with medication. Culture is the bloodstream of your organization. Before you can use it wisely and purposefully, you must understand it. How much do you know about your culture? Have you ever had a cultural audit or assessment? Can you describe your organizational culture in a single sentence? Can you list some of the key traditions of your organizational culture? Is there any wet work going on? Do you have termites?

These are important questions relevant to not only the CEO and the C-Suite but also every organizational member. If are going to change and improve organizational culture, you have to know where you are so you can assess the length and breadth of your journey to your desired destination.

Culture will make or break any effort at transforming your organization into an ethically intelligent organization. Find out if you have the Sick Six cultural dysfunctions. Satisfy yourself that your values statements translate into values behaviors. Please know that posting a survey on Survey Monkey and having your team members respond is not going to answer the questions I've posed. A doctor is needed to diagnose illness in people. Likewise, a doctor is needed to diagnose organizational cultural illnesses. We can help. Just ask.

Cloister. In Chapter 8, we discussed the Captivity Cloister and Innocuous Imperial Box, metaphorical structures within which we confine members of the C-Suite. As much as is practical, dismantle those structures. As enticing as the idea of squeezing every nanosecond of productivity out of your highly paid C-Suite leaders may be, there are serious downsides, as I described in Chapter 8. Yes, provide all of the assistants and tools necessary for maximizing productivity, but tear down the walls of isolation and captivity. Get your C-Suite members out into the organization. Everyone might be surprised at what they learn. Spread the same practice into other areas of the organization.

> ... tear down the walls of isolation and captivity. Get your C-Suite members out into the organization.

I once consulted with the CEO of a manufacturing organization about commercialization of engineering ideas or, in their case, the lack thereof. This CEO, who was an engineer, described an elaborate internal process for moving newly discovered engineering breakthroughs into the marketing arena for commercialization. Unfortunately, there was little commercialization because the marketing group always found a reason why the "breakthroughs" wouldn't succeed in the marketplace. After some investigation, I discovered the engineering group was sequestered in an engineering lab located some miles from headquarters, where the marketing group was situated.

When I asked the CEO the reason for the separation of these two groups, he was surprised that the logic of it had escaped me. His response was, "I want to keep those guys [the engineers] focused on their jobs. I don't want them wandering around the halls of headquarters wasting their time. I especially don't want them talking to the marketing guys. They would just fill the heads of my engineers with all their cockamamie ideas. No, it was a stroke of genius on my part keeping my engineers away from all those harebrained marketing types. I want my sales and marketing people focused on selling, and my engineers focused on research and development."

Do you recognize the problem?

This organization needed collaboration, not segregation. I recommended that the marketing organization and the engineering group communicate frequently, even working together on projects. Imagine the time that was saved when an engineer with an idea ran it by a marketing or sales person who either validated it or killed it before the organization wasted substantial resources. Organizations that create walls and stovepipes will not survive the relentless competition of the 24/7/365 21st century business environment.

I had another client that did the same thing with their information technology group. At great expense, the information technology group was relocated, in this case, across town from the users they were supporting. Over time, help-desk response times increased, and the user-friendliness of applications degenerated. After talking to the information technology folks and the users, it was clear the separation was responsible for the problems.

When everyone was together in one location, informal conversations and day-to-day activities created a symbiotic relationship between the information technology group and users. The physical separation had built walls of ignorance and indifference that previously didn't exist.

Tear down those walls. Yes, there are instances where secrecy and information must be compartmentalized and released only to those with a need to know. But unless you lead a spy agency or a team creating the next cutting-edge weapons system for the Department of Defense, those walls and stovepipes are costing you dearly. Insist on horizontal as well as vertical communications.

Spend some time walking around and talking to people in your manufacturing plant or call center. Go on some sales calls with your sales team and find out what your customers are actually saying about your organization and your products and/or services. You may learn that Otherness is not necessarily hostile.

> Ethically intelligent organizations engage in strategic openness rooted in wisdom.

Otherness. Test your assumptions about others. Keep your Worldview Window clear. Ethically intelligent organizations engage in strategic openness rooted in wisdom. Think back to our discussions of Violative Paranoia and Hostile Otherness. That paranoia and hostility is real. I understand the defensive reactions to it. But not everyone is out to get us. Not every interaction with our external environment is fraught with great danger. Strategic openness is something all living organisms use to survive. With non-sentient organisms, it's autonomic. Instinctual interactions with the external environment are saturated with caution and fear. But they, nonetheless, occur. With humans, strategic openness must be interwoven with acknowledged fear, informed caution and learned wisdom.

Strategic openness must permeate your organizational culture. Almost everyone in your organization is going to interact with your external environment. Not all of those interactions can be monitored or screened by your legal department. Well, I take that back. It's possible for your legal department to monitor and screen every external interaction, but you'll go out of business waiting for something to happen.

I understand there are risks in encouraging organizational members to engage in strategic openness. I've worked in one of the most highly regulated industries in the country. But with proper training and supervision, strategic openness can work to your benefit. A companion solution is reform.

Reform

There is much in business and government needing reform, none more urgently than the Foreign Corrupt Practices Act and Regulation Full Disclosure. I've already addressed both of these well-intentioned but harmful responses to real-world problems. There are some additional points I want to address and amplify others.

Foreign Corrupt Practices Act (FCPA). The FCPA is a source of civic corruption and an enabling force for foreign competition. The FCPA was an ill-fated attempt to export our view of pristine business competition to the rest of the world. I'll let you decide if that is a noble enterprise or not. But despite FCPA promoters' claims that it's working because our view is slowly being recognized and adopted worldwide, the reality is that FCPA not only restrains United States-based companies' ability to compete effectively in worldwide markets but also aids and abets our foreign competitors. Our senior business leadership won't criticize the law for fear of political repercussions. I'll dare to speak for them and make the politically incorrect statement—this is nuts! Companies headquartered in the United States spend untold billions of dollars complying with FCPA and its accompanying regulations. This law has taken management of the foreign operations of United States companies out of the hands of experienced operational leaders and transferred it to lawyers. Legal counsel for these companies are paranoid about this law and its regulations. As result, they go to extreme measures hoping not to violate its Byzantine mosaic. This law is suffocating the foreign operations of our domestic companies with scant return on investment.

Here's an example. I was recently talking to an executive of a Fortune 100 company domiciled in the United States. We were reminiscing about how much easier it was to do business overseas 25 years ago. In those days, if a country manager needed $500 to ease the passage of machinery through customs, you would simply approve with no questions asked. This executive told me that, these days, he wouldn't even attempt the $500 payment because he would incur over $5,000 in compliance expense trying to make the $500 happen. His firm would simply put up with the foreign "bureaucratic delays" and eat the cost of the wasted time as a cost of doing business. Incidentally, the cost of the wasted time was far in excess of the $500 "passage" payment.

As I said at the beginning, this is not only nuts, but it's also hypocritical. Foreign executives look at what we do, and they think we're crazy. We're not only less competitive by tying our own hands behind our back, but we also think we're furthering our pristine view of competitive practices in foreign cultures.

Nothing could be further from the truth. Foreign executives look at our domestic practices when dealing with governmental agencies and see nothing superior to the practices in their own cultures. They pay to grease the wheels of commerce, and we call it bribery. We pay to grease the wheels of commerce in the United States, and we call it political contributions. Foreign business executives call that hypocrisy.

> They pay to grease the wheels of commerce, and we call it bribery. We pay to grease the wheels of commerce in the United States, and we call it political contributions.

The FCPA and its ensnaring regulations need to be thrown into the dustbin of history. Let our companies compete when operating in foreign markets. We have no business trying to forcibly export our business practices into other cultures. If our business practices are superior, that superiority should be revealed on the field of competition, not in the bowels of government bureaucracies and courtrooms. Don't get me wrong, I'm not advocating bribing government officials. But we need to recognize that, in some cultures, the income of low-level government bureaucrats is like the income of wait staff in the United States. The salary is low, but the difference is earned in tips. Our business leaders should be able to pay those tips without the fear of going to prison.

The FCPA, among many other laws and regulations, is corroding and corrupting the relationship between government and business. It has caused a corrosive cloud of hostility to descend into our domestic business environment, birthing a commonly held view of government as the hostile Other. Our businesses have reacted by forming political action committees that make billions of dollars of political contributions in an attempt at allaying the hostility. When organized crime engages in this sort of activity, we call it a protection racket and label it a crime. We must find an ethically intelligent solution to this sordid consequence. Regulation Full Disclosure, another well intended law, has had similar unintended consequences.

Regulation Full Disclosure (FD). Because I covered Regulation Full Disclosure (FD) in some detail in Chapter 8, I'm not going to repeat that discussion here. My purpose here is to make the case for reforming this regulation in a way that permits senior business leaders a well-defined exit from their solitary confinement. The intent of Regulation FD is noble. It was aimed at reducing insider trading. The jury is still out whether this objective has been obtained. There is no doubt, however, about the serious undesirable unintended consequences of this regulation. We've made it nearly impossible for senior business leaders to have practical and meaningful outside lifelines.

There have been some accommodations offered. Senior business leaders have a narrow safe harbor of individuals with whom they can have "privileged" conversations. For many of the reasons we have already discussed, the safe harbor is too narrow. The limited audience with whom a senior business leader is permitted to have conversations is impractical and unworkable. Why? Lawyers are rightly paranoid. Although the regulation permits certain types of conversations, out of an abundance of caution: Most corporate legal counsels would prefer *no* conversations. The contents of a conversation can't be misconstrued if the conversation never takes place. I completely understand that logic. Corporate legal counsels are only doing their jobs.

The real solution to this problem is a generous safe harbor along the lines of the secret meeting I described at the beginning of Chapter 8. These illicit meetings are now taking place. We should make them legal. There are plenty of public-minded social organizations that could easily host these types of meetings.

Senior business leaders are serious and responsible members of the community. The probability of any of them trying to profit from the sort of intimate information shared in these meetings is very low. On the other hand, potential rewards to society at large are huge. As the percentage of senior business leaders carrying the Essential Credential grows, the rewards would be even greater.

Essential Credential

In the final chapter of this book, we'll discuss why ethical intelligence is the foundation of leadership. Managers and leaders should not presume to lead others until they have shown they are ethically intelligent, or at least on the journey to becoming ethically intelligent.

Leadership is a sacred bond. It's a special relationship between leader and follower that is grounded in mutual trust and respect. We should demand the highest ethical standards from our managers and leaders. In that regard, I have a dream and a vision for the future of leadership.

I have a vision that one day every manager and leader will possess a Heart-Mind Map and certificate demonstrating a fluent ethical intelligence—an Essential Credential. As we gather more data and create hundreds, perhaps thousands of Heart-Mind Maps, we'll be able to statistically create and validate a "normal" or "standard." The point is, those who seek to manage and lead others must show, in some way, that they possess the ethical intelligence to deserve our trust. *You cannot lead without it.*

———————◆———————

Chapter Highlights

- Let's stop locking the barn door after the horse is gone.
- Hermeneutic-phenomenological analysis shows great promise.
- Heart-Mind Maps convert the ephemeral and subjective into a form more easily grasped and understood.

- Lying is an insidious poison to any organizational culture. It corrodes the very essence of trust.
- Hire and nurture ethically intelligent people.
- Ethically intelligent organizations are places where telling the truth is the number one value.
- People who do what's right in all circumstances are the backbone of a right-thinking-right-acting organization.
- Great managers and leaders are great actors. They show us. They lift us with their example. They inspire us with actions. They walk the talk.
- Culture is the life force that animates organizations. It transforms ephemeral missions and vision into reality.
- Culture is the conduit for transfusing ethical intelligence into your organization.
- Ethically intelligent organizations engage in strategic openness rooted in wisdom.
- Foreign business executives pay to grease the wheels of commerce, and we call it bribery. Domestic business leaders pay to grease the wheels of commerce in the United States, and we call it political contributions.
- One day every manager and leader will possess a Heart-Mind Map and certificate demonstrating a fluent ethical intelligence—an Essential Credential.

Questions for You

- Is your organization ethically intelligent?
- Is truth-telling the number one value in your organization?
- Can you describe your organizational culture in one sentence?
- When was the last time you just showed up at an operating unit?
- Are your internal processes discerning?
- When was your last cultural assessment?
- Is your board ethically intelligent?

ABOUT THE AUTHOR

Dr. John Opincar, CPA, CGMA, serves as President and CEO of Boardroom Partners, a board-level consultancy. He is a college professor and President and CEO of the Ethical Intelligence Research Center, a not-for-profit research and educational institute. His current professional pursuits are all directed toward making the world a better place through research, writing, speaking and teaching about team-based corporate governance and human ethical intelligence—one person and one organization at a time.

Previously, Dr. Opincar served as Campus and Academic Director for the University of Phoenix in Iowa. Since joining the University of Phoenix in 2003, he also served as Director of Academic Affairs in Iowa, Lead Faculty/Area Chair in Houston, and Associate Faculty member in Iowa, Houston, and Online Campuses. Dr. Opincar continues his role as a University of Phoenix associate faculty member. He previously held teaching posts at Belhaven University and Our Lady of the Lake University.

Prior to entering higher education, Dr. Opincar built a successful multi-decade career in business with large enterprises such as Deloitte Touche, PriceWaterhouseCoopers, and Ford Motor Company. He also founded and led several startups, the last of which was housed in the Technology Incubator at the University of Texas at Austin.

During his career, Dr. Opincar served in numerous business and higher educational leadership positions, including Chief Academic Officer at the University of Phoenix, CFO of a NYSE energy company, managing director of an international software consortium, board member and advisor, senior consultant to a select group of Fortune 500 clients and their directors and CEO of a number of privately held companies.

Dr. Opincar earned degrees from the University of Detroit Mercy, Michigan State University and the University of Phoenix. He is a lifetime member of Alpha Sigma Nu, Beta Alpha Psi, Beta Gamma Sigma and Delta Mu Delta honor societies. Dr. Opincar is a Certified Public Accountant in Michigan and a Chartered Global Management Accountant. He is a certified John Maxwell Team leadership coach, trainer and speaker. His non-professional pursuits include gourmet cooking, music, politics, gardening and Standard Poodles.

Author's Contact Information
Boardroom Partners, Inc.
346-444-2626
john.opincar@boardroompartners.com

www.ingramcontent.com/pod-product-compliance
Lightning Source LLC
Chambersburg PA
CBHW020302030426
42336CB00010B/872